AC
MILAN

by Todd Kortemeier

SportsZone

An Imprint of Abdo Publishing
abdopublishing.com

EUROPE'S BEST
SOCCER CLUBS

abdopublishing.com

Published by Abdo Publishing, a division of ABDO, PO Box 398166, Minneapolis, Minnesota 55439. Copyright © 2018 by Abdo Consulting Group, Inc. International copyrights reserved in all countries. No part of this book may be reproduced in any form without written permission from the publisher. SportsZone™ is a trademark and logo of Abdo Publishing.

Printed in the United States of America, North Mankato, Minnesota
042017
092017

Cover Photo: Luca Bruno/AP Images, foreground; Carlo Fumagalli/AP Images, background
Interior Photos: Bas Czerwinski/AP Images, 4; Alberto Pellaschiar/AP Images, 7, 24; Scott Heppell/AP Images, 9; Thanassis Stavrakis/AP Images, 11; Jon Super/AP Images, 12; Carlo Fumagalli/AP Images, 14; Keystone/Hulton Archive/Getty Images, 17; Popperfoto/Getty Images, 18, 30; Luca Bruno/AP Images, 21, 22, 27; Staff/AFP/Getty Images, 28; Rudi Blaha/AP Images, 33; Allsport UK/Getty Images Sport/Getty Images, 35; Antonio Calanni/AP Images, 36, 38, 43; Michael Sohn/AP Images, 40

Editor: Patrick Donnelly
Series Designer: Craig Hinton
Content Consultant: Paul Logothetis, European soccer reporter

Publisher's Cataloging-in-Publication Data

Names: Kortemeier, Todd, author.
Title: AC Milan / by Todd Kortemeier.
Description: Minneapolis, MN : Abdo Publishing, 2018. | Series: Europe's best
    soccer clubs | Includes bibliographical references and index.
Identifiers: LCCN 2016963084 | ISBN 9781532111297 (lib. bdg.) |
    ISBN 9781680789140 (ebook)
Subjects: LCSH: Soccer--Europe--History--Juvenile literature. | Soccer teams--
    Europe--History--Juvenile literature. | Soccer--Europe--Records--Juvenile
    literature. | Associazione Calcio Milan (Soccer team)--Juvenile literature.
Classification: DDC 796.334--dc23
LC record available at http://lccn.loc.gov/2016963084

TABLE OF
CONTENTS

CHAPTER 1

CHAMPIONS OF EUROPE

In the summer of 2006, AC Milan's fans were looking forward to a historic season. The club had finished second in Serie A, Italy's top league. It also had beaten out its biggest rival, Internazionale, also known as Inter Milan, or simply Inter. Now it needed to take the next step and win a trophy or two.

But then everything changed. A scandal rocked the Italian soccer world. Defending Serie A champion Juventus and other teams were accused of trying to influence which referees would officiate their games. Milan was one of the clubs accused of cheating. It was given a 15-point penalty in the standings.

And it wouldn't be allowed to play in the Union of European Football Associations (UEFA) Champions League.

Milan challenged the punishment. The Italian Football Federation agreed to reduce the penalty to eight points. And Milan was let back into the Champions League. But it had to start in an earlier round. And the points penalty still made it harder to qualify for the Champions League the next season.

Sticking Together

But the players were determined to succeed. They gathered for training early. Some of them had just finished playing in the World Cup. Five Milan players were on the Italian team that had won it all, including defender Alessandro Nesta, midfielders Gennaro Gattuso and Andrea Pirlo, and forwards Filippo Inzaghi and Alberto Gilardino. On Milan they joined other stars including defender and captain Paolo Maldini, midfielder Clarence Seedorf, and forward Kaká. They were united as a team to overcome the challenges.

FAST FACT

Despite the eight-point penalty, Milan ended up finishing fourth in Serie A in 2006–07. That was good enough to qualify for the Champions League again the next year.

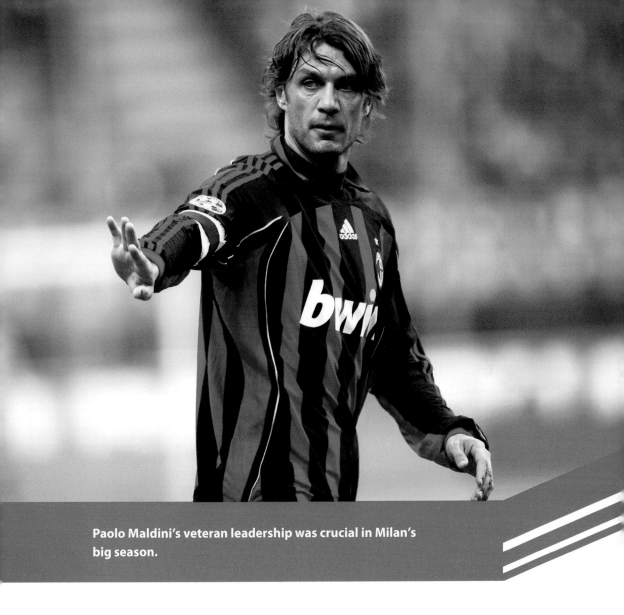

Paolo Maldini's veteran leadership was crucial in Milan's big season.

The league schedule was difficult. Milan at one point lost three home games in a row. That hadn't happened in 40 years. In the Champions League, Milan narrowly beat Red Star Belgrade to qualify for the group stage. There, it played the three other teams in its group twice. Milan was undefeated

EUROPEAN SOCCER

The European soccer season is broken down into different levels of competition. It can be confusing to keep track of it all. Here's a handy guide to help you follow the action.

League Play

The 20 best teams in Italy play in Serie A. Teams play all league opponents twice each season for 38 total games. The three teams with the worst records are relegated—or sent down—to Serie B, which sends its top three teams up to replace them the next season. Serie A was officially founded in 1898. It has operated in its current format of each team playing the others twice since 1929.

European Play

The top three teams in Serie A qualify for the UEFA Champions League. This annual tournament involves the best teams from the top leagues throughout Europe. The Champions League debuted in 1992. It replaced the European Cup, a similar tournament that began in 1955.

The next three teams from Serie A qualify for the UEFA Europa League. The Europa League is Europe's second-tier tournament. It runs in a similar manner to the Champions League but crowns its own winner. The Europa League debuted in 1971 as the UEFA Cup but was renamed Europa League in 2009.

Domestic Cups

Teams from the top four levels of Italian soccer are eligible to play in the *Coppa Italia* or Italian Cup. Nearly 80 teams from Serie A through Serie D can enter. Founded in 1922, the tournament consists of eight rounds over two phases. The highest-ranked Serie A teams enter at the Round of 16.

Alberto Gilardino plays the ball against Celtic in a Champions League match at Glasgow, Scotland.

through four games. Although it lost the last two, Milan had done enough to advance to the knockout round.

Milan played Scottish champions Celtic over two games in the round of 16. The first was a scoreless draw on the road in Glasgow. Back home in Italy, a goal in extra time sent Milan through. In the next round against Germany's Bayern Munich, Milan again tied on the road before winning at home. The semifinal saw Milan lose the first match to English foe

Manchester United 3–2. But a 3–0 rout back in Milan clinched a place in the final.

Revenge

The 2007 Champions League final was a single match played in Athens, Greece, against English rival Liverpool. It was a rematch of the 2005 final. Liverpool came out on top that night.

But this time Milan had other ideas. One player who hadn't forgotten that loss was Inzaghi, who didn't get a chance to play in 2005. He had to watch as Milan blew a 3–0 halftime lead and lost on penalty kicks.

At the age of 33, Inzaghi was a bit of a surprise to start the 2007 final. But the move looked like genius when he deflected in the game's first goal just before halftime.

Both teams had their chances in the second half. Milan forward Kaká was one of the best playmakers in the world. That showed in the final when he set up the winning goal.

FAST FACT

Later in 2007 Milan won the Club World Cup against the champions of other continents. Milan beat Boca Juniors from Argentina 4–2 in the final.

Inzaghi beats Liverpool goalkeeper Pepe Reina to score Milan's second goal in the Champions League final.

Kaká picked out Inzaghi with a pass. Inzaghi dribbled around Liverpool goalkeeper Pepe Reina. Then he sent the ball underneath the sprawling keeper and into the net.

But even with a 2–0 lead, Milan wasn't able to relax. Memories of that blown lead in 2005 were still fresh. In the last minute of regular time, Liverpool's Daniel Agger sent in a corner kick. Dirk Kuyt headed the ball in, closing the gap to one goal. But Milan was able to control stoppage time and see the match out. It was the seventh Champions League title for Milan. Only Real Madrid of Spain had won more.

A picture of captain Maldini hoisting the trophy was splashed across most Italian newspapers. The headlines gave credit to Inzaghi, the man nicknamed "Super Pippo." He credited the team sticking together as a major reason they overcame so many challenges.

"We wouldn't have done so had we not been so close," Inzaghi said.

Maldini, center, and his teammates celebrate their Champions League title.

Swedish trio Gunnar Gren, Gunnar Nordahl, and Nils Liedholm starred for AC Milan in the 1950s.

CHAPTER 2

I ROSSONERI

O ver the years, AC Milan has become one of Italy's most famous soccer clubs. But when it began, it was a soccer and cricket club. It was founded by two Englishmen, Alfred Edwards and Herbert Kilpin. They started Milan Cricket and Foot-Ball Club on December 16, 1899. The club's current name honors its English roots. Milan is the English spelling of the city's name. In Italy the city is known as *Milano*.

Edwards was the club's first president. He entered the team into the Italian Football Federation in January. In the 1900–01 season, Milan captured its first national league title.

Milan was the dominant team in the region throughout much of the decade. That changed in 1908 when a split in the club gave rise to its biggest rival. A group of AC Milan members thought the club should have more foreign players. So they formed their own team. They named it Internazionale, meaning "international" in English. Today that team is often referred to as Inter Milan, or simply Inter.

Home Sweet Home

Milan didn't win a title during the next 40 seasons. But while the club didn't make many advances on the field, it did build a new one. On September 19, 1926, Milan played its first game at San Siro Stadium. It took its name from a nearby church named for Saint Siro.

In the first game, Milan lost a friendly to Inter 6–3. Although Milan would eventually share the stadium with Inter, Milan had the San Siro to itself in the early years. Despite the team's struggles, Milan fans continued to

FAST FACT

Milan has worn its famous red and black colors since the club was founded. The team is often referred to as the *Rossoneri*—a combination of the Italian words for "red" and "black."

San Siro Stadium is packed for a game in the 1950s.

pack the San Siro. By 1935, the 35,000-seat capacity wasn't nearly enough. The stadium was modified and reached a peak capacity of 85,000 in 1955.

By that time, Milan was back among the top teams of Italy. Swedish star Gunnar Nordahl joined Milan in 1949 and led the league with 35 goals. The next season, Milan won its fourth league championship. Nordahl continued to dominate, and Milan won two more league titles in the 1950s.

European Success

Four league titles in 10 years established Milan as one of Italy's best teams. But one title was missing. The European Cup was

created in 1955 to determine the best club team in Europe. In 1963 Milan became the first Italian team to win the European Cup (now called the Champions League), beating Benfica of Portugal 2–1 in the final. It won its second European Cup in 1969 on the strength of a Pierino Prati hat trick against Dutch club Ajax in a 4–1 victory.

But Milan soon entered another down period. It won just one league title from 1968 to 1988. Perhaps the lowest point in club history was from 1980 to 1983. The team was relegated to a lower division on two separate occasions, the first due to a match-fixing scandal that affected seven teams. Milan responded both times by winning the Serie B title in its first try and getting back into Serie A.

Captains Cesare Maldini, left, of Milan and Mario Coluna of Benfica meet before the 1963 European Cup final.

Investing in Success

Milan's best years were just ahead. In 1986 controversial billionaire

Silvio Berlusconi purchased the club. The media mogul and future Prime Minister of Italy gave out big contracts to top players such as scoring sensation Marco van Basten and hired coach Arrigo Sacchi. Van Basten was from the Netherlands, a country known for attacking soccer. Combined with a tough defense, Milan was impressive to watch.

Milan won back-to-back European Cups in 1989 and 1990. Through 2016 Milan was the last club to have successfully defended its title. In 1990 Italy hosted the World Cup. The San Siro was one of the stadiums used. Italy finished third in the tournament, thanks in part to the efforts of four Milan players.

Manager Fabio Capello took over for Sacchi in 1991. The club didn't miss a beat. In fact, it hardly ever got beat. Milan won 58 league games in a row after Capello took over. It also won three league titles in a row and another Champions League in 1994.

After Capello's final league title in 1996, the club had mixed success. It took some new stars to get Milan back to the top.

Manager Arrigo Sacchi and striker Marco van Basten embrace after leading Milan to victory in the 1989 European Cup final.

CHAPTER 3

WORLDWIDE ACCLAIM

There's an old saying: Keep your friends close and your enemies closer. AC Milan couldn't keep Internazionale much closer. The two rivals share San Siro Stadium.

In Italian the rivalry is known as the *Derby della Madonnina*. The Madonnina is a famous statue in Milan. In English the rivalry is usually known as the Milan Derby. The teams have battled each other for more than a century. Historically, Milan represented working-class people. Internazionale fans typically lived in the wealthier parts of the city. Those distinctions have

Rival players look on as firefighters attempt to control the flames at a 2005 Champions League game between Milan and Inter.

changed over the years. But the fans are no less passionate about their teams.

The two clubs have often battled each other for the Serie A title. The rivalry took off in the 1960s as both teams became two-time champions of Europe. Over the years, the two have met several times in elimination games. The 1977 final of the Coppa Italia was the first one. The Coppa Italia is a tournament for all soccer teams in Italy. Milan beat Inter 2–0.

Champions League Drama

Perhaps the biggest meetings of the clubs have come in the Champions League. In 2002–03, Inter and Milan were two of the four clubs left. They met in the semifinals. Because it was a two-leg round, both matches were at the San Siro. The first leg was a home game for Milan. It ended 0–0. The second leg was another draw, this time 1–1. But because Milan had scored more "away" goals, it advanced to the final, where it beat another Italian power, Juventus.

A Champions League rematch in 2005 descended into violence. Inter fans were upset their team was losing. They threw flares that started grass fires on the field. The match had to be called off and Milan was declared the winner. Inter was fined and had to play its next four matches with no fans in attendance.

Violence has no place in soccer, but fans are expected to be passionate. AC Milan's most passionate fans set up

FAST FACT

A nickname for Milan fans is *Casciavit*. In Italian it means "screwdriver." This term was used by Inter fans who looked down on Milan fans for being lower-class workers. But Milan fans embraced the term as a source of pride in their roots.

behind one of the goals at the San Siro. They make colorful displays and signs. They also chant and sing. One of Milan's famous songs is called *Inno Milan*. One of its verses translates to, "With Milan in our hearts / In the depths of our soul / You're a true friend / And together we sing."

Worldwide Attraction

A 2015 survey determined that Milan was the third most popular team in Italy. Yet it is also one of the top 10 most popular clubs in Europe. The club also has fans all over the world. In 2016 it played a series of friendly matches in the United States. Its match against English club Chelsea in Minnesota drew more than 64,000 fans. Milan has hundreds of official supporters clubs spread over five continents.

The club has some famous fans, including former National Basketball Association star Kobe Bryant. Bryant spent part of his childhood in Italy when his dad played pro basketball

FAST FACT

In 2015 Milan considered replacing the San Siro. The new stadium would be smaller and move fans closer to the action. But the team decided to remain at the San Siro. The stadium underwent improvements in preparation for hosting the 2016 Champions League final.

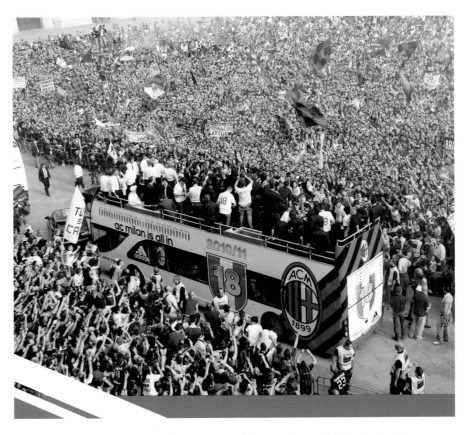

Milan fans pack the streets in 2011 to celebrate the club's 18th Serie A title.

there. Other celebrity supporters include top tennis champion Novak Djokovic and Formula One driver Felipe Massa.

AC Milan has a proud history. It has many dedicated fans and great players. Since its founding in 1899, the club has become one of the best in the world. It has won many titles and played exciting soccer for its fans. *Rossoneri* fans hope that will continue for generations to come.

CHAPTER 4

Nils Liedholm was one of three great Swedish players to make a name for himself in Milan.

STARS OF THE PAST

Since David Allison scored Milan's first goal in 1900, the club has had many stars. Louis Van Hege was one of the first. He led the club in the early 1900s, averaging more than one goal per match. After a long stretch without much success, Gunnar Nordahl changed the club's fortunes for good. When he arrived in Milan in 1949, the club hadn't won a title in more than 40 years. A few months earlier, Nordahl had won an Olympic gold medal with Sweden. He was at the top of his game.

Nordahl led Serie A in goals five times. He is still the club's all-time scoring leader with 221 goals. He and fellow Swedes

Gunnar Gren and Nils Liedholm brought Milan back to the top. The three players were known as "Gre-No-Li."

Stars of Europe

Homegrown heroes also have found success with the *Rossoneri*. Defender Cesare Maldini came to Milan in 1954. He first played at right back. But he later moved to center back because of his ability to shut down opponents. Maldini was the captain of the first Milan team to win the European Cup in 1963.

FAST FACT

Milan has honored two of its greatest players by retiring their uniform numbers. The No. 6 of Franco Baresi and the No. 3 of Paolo Maldini are both retired. Maldini said that if one of his sons plays for Milan, he could wear No. 3.

Jose Altafini was an even bigger part of the European Cup victory. The Brazilian forward was 20 when he came to Milan in 1958. He immediately led Serie A in scoring with 28 goals. He was a strong, powerful runner who used both feet equally well. Altafini scored two goals in the 1963 European Cup final.

Gianni Rivera poses with Brazilian legend Pelé before a 1963 game.

In Italy it's not enough to play well. Fans love players who have style. Gianni Rivera was one of Milan's most stylish players. He first wore the red and black in 1960 at the age of 17. He never played for another club. In 1969 he became the first Italian player to win the Ballon d'Or (French for "Golden Ball"), given to the best player in Europe. Nicknamed "Golden Boy," Rivera helped Milan win multiple European and league titles.

Three Dutchmen Lead the Way

Like Gre-No-Li in the 1950s, a trio of outsiders helped Milan to reach new heights in the 1980s. This time it was three Dutchmen. Playmakers Ruud Gullit and Marco van Basten arrived in Milan in 1987. Defender/midfielder Frank Rijkaard signed a year later. The three were a nearly unbeatable combo.

Rijkaard started attacks with his defense. He could play in front of the line of defenders and smartly deploy the ball. Gullit was the creative force. His playmaking ability meant he could make great passes

FAST FACT

Franco Baresi is the longest-serving captain in Milan history. He held the job from 1982 to 1997. Milan had only four captains between 1982 and 2013, when Riccardo Montolivo assumed the captain's armband.

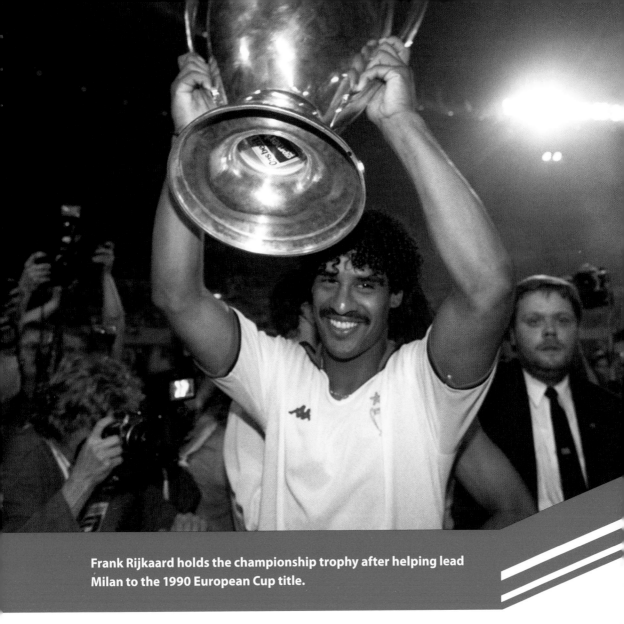

Frank Rijkaard holds the championship trophy after helping lead Milan to the 1990 European Cup title.

through to the forwards. Then it was up to van Basten. He was extremely accurate and powerful with his shots.

The Dutchmen played together until 1993. In that time they won three Serie A titles and two more European championships.

The European Cup victories came back-to-back in 1989 and 1990 under the guidance of manager Arrigo Sacchi. In the 1989 finals, van Basten and Gullit each scored two goals in a 4–0 rout of Romanian club Steaua Bucharest. Rijkaard had his turn as hero in the 1990 win. He scored the only goal of the final as Milan nipped Benfica.

The era from 1986 to 1996 was the greatest in Milan's history. The club won titles but also played beautifully. The Milan teams of this era were known as "The Immortals." Even as the Dutch trio departed, they left behind a strong team. Some of the club's lesser-known stars hit their peak in the mid-1990s.

In 1994 Milan destroyed Spanish giant Barcelona in the Champions League final 4–0. The *Rossoneri* added another Serie A title in 1996. But after that, the club went into another slight decline. Fans anxiously awaited their next generation of stars.

Ruud Gullit starred for Milan from 1987 to 1994.

CHAPTER 5

MODERN STARS

The names "Maldini" and "Milan" are intertwined throughout Italian soccer history. Maldini is the most famous name in club history. First it was for Cesare, former captain and later manager of Milan. Then his son Paolo became an even bigger legend.

Paolo Maldini debuted at halftime of a 1985 Serie A match when he was just 16 years old. He never played for another club. The defender racked up more than 900 appearances for Milan in 25 seasons. It's no coincidence that this era featured some of

Andrea Pirlo scores on a penalty kick in 2002.

the best Milan teams ever. Maldini won seven Serie A titles and
five European championships.

The trophies were numerous. But it was his presence on
the field that fans remember. He was a calm, cool player and a

defensive force. Maldini was named Milan's captain in 1997. He kept the title until his retirement in 2009.

Pirlo's Impact

Andrea Pirlo saw both sides of the Milan rivalry. He started his career with Inter. But he moved to Milan in 2001 and soon made a big impact. Pirlo led the club to a Champions League title in 2003. The next season, Milan won the Serie A title. Pirlo was a playmaking midfielder. He made 401 total appearances in 10 seasons with the *Rossoneri*.

International Strike Force

Milan was loaded with talent in the 2000s. Ukrainian Andriy Shevchenko threatened Gunnar Nordahl with his scoring pace. Shevchenko recorded 175 goals in 324 games. He retired in second place on the club career scoring list. Brazilian Kaká spent

FAST FACT

Carlo Ancelotti appeared as a midfielder in 112 matches for Milan from 1987 to 1992. Then he led the club to two Champions League titles in an eight-year run as manager from 2001 to 2009.

six years in Milan. His speed on attacking runs made him one of the best in the world.

Clarence Seedorf continued Milan's proud history of Dutch players. His strong play at midfield helped Milan win the Champions League in 2003 and 2007.

Milan still had several Italian stars during this era. Longtime midfielder Gennaro Gattuso was Milan's stopper. His bold challenges and deft tackles helped make sure no opponent could get through easily. Defender Alessandro Nesta and forward Filippo Inzaghi played big roles as well.

A New Era

Milan's win in the 2007 Club World Cup was its 18th international title. That set a world record. A new manager, Massimiliano Allegri, brought the *Rossoneri* a Serie A title in 2011. Though he only played at Milan from 2010 to 2012, Swedish striker Zlatan Ibrahimovic had a huge impact on those teams. He scored 56 goals in two seasons.

Milan has had strong goalkeepers in its history. But none had such an early start as Gianluigi Donnarumma.

Andriy Shevchenko gets past a Juventus defender at the 2003 Champions League final.

The Italian made his Milan debut in 2015 at age 16. He was the youngest goalkeeper ever to start a match in Serie A. He quickly became Milan's full-time starter and one of the best keepers in the league. He's even earned a spot on Italy's national team.

If you see a red and black blur on the right of Milan's defense, it's probably Ignazio Abate. The speedy Italian fullback made his debut in the 2009–10 season. He quickly became one of the best defenders in Serie A. Besides his speed, his passing and crossing ability helps set up teammates to score.

In 2013 Riccardo Montolivo was named Milan's newest captain. He earned the honor after one season with the club. The Italian midfielder quickly became a force in Milan's lineup. Milan's young but promising roster inspired hopes of a return to greatness for the *Rossoneri*.

Young goalkeeper Gianluigi Donnarumma was already a star as a teenager with Milan.

AC MILAN
TEAM FILE

FULL NAME: Associazione Calcio Milan

YEAR FORMED: 1899

WHERE THEY PLAY: San Siro Stadium, Milan, Italy

SERIE A TITLES: 18
(most recent 2010–11)

COPPA ITALIA TITLES: 5
(most recent 2002–03)

EUROPEAN CUP/CHAMPIONS LEAGUE TITLES: 7
(most recent 2006–07)

KEY RECORDS

- Most appearances: Paolo Maldini, 902

- Most goals: Gunnar Nordahl, 221

- Youngest goal scorer: Gianni Rivera, 17 years, 80 days

- Biggest margin of victory in a Serie A match: 9–0 v. Palermo, November 18, 1951

AUTHOR'S DREAM TEAM

GOALKEEPER: Sebastiano Rossi

DEFENSE: Paolo Maldini, Frank Rijkaard, Franco Baresi, Alessandro Costacurta

MIDFIELD: Nils Liedholm, Andrea Pirlo, Kaká, Gianni Rivera

FORWARDS: Gunnar Nordahl, Andriy Shevchenko

TIMELINE

1899

AC Milan is founded as Milan Cricket and Foot-Ball Club.

1901

Milan wins its first league title.

1908

A dispute over foreign players causes Milan members to form a rival team, known as Internazionale.

1926

AC Milan opens its current home, San Siro Stadium.

1951

On the strength of Gunnar Nordahl's goal scoring, Milan wins its first league title since 1907.

1963

Milan beats Benfica for its first European Cup title.

1980

Milan is relegated to Serie B for the first time in club history.

1990

A trio of Dutch stars leads Milan to its second consecutive European Cup.

2003

Milan defeats Juventus 3–2 on penalty kicks after a scoreless 120 minutes in the first all-Italian Champions League final.

2007

Milan rebounds from an eight-point penalty to win the Champions League.

2011

Milan wins its 18th Serie A title.

2015

Goalkeeper Gianluigi Donnarumma makes his debut with Milan at age 16.

GLOSSARY

corner kick

When a team is awarded a free kick from a corner of the field near the opponent's goal.

cross

A pass delivered from the side of the field toward the middle.

debut

First appearance.

derby

A rivalry game in soccer.

forward

A soccer player who plays close to the opponent's goal and usually scores goals.

friendly

A match that doesn't count in the regular standings.

fullback

A defensive soccer player usually positioned toward one side of the field.

hat trick

Three goals scored in one game by the same player.

match fixing

Illegally attempting to affect the outcome of a match.

relegated

When a soccer team is demoted from a higher league to a lower league.

stoppage time

Time added on to the end of the half to make up for time the ball was out of play.

tackle

A defensive move to try and take the ball away from another player.

FOR MORE INFORMATION

BOOKS

Hoena, Blake. *Everything Soccer*. Washington, DC: National Geographic Society, 2014.

Jones, Jeremy V. *Toward the Goal: The Kaká Story*. Grand Rapids, MI: Zonderkidz, 2014.

Whiting, Jim. *AC Milan*. Mankato, MN: Creative Education, 2016.

WEBSITES

To learn more about AC Milan, visit abdobooklinks.com. These links are routinely monitored and updated to provide the most current information available.

PLACE TO VISIT

CASA MILAN
Via Aldo Rossi, 8 20149 Milan, Italy
Phone: +39 02 62284545
casamilan.acmilan.com/en

Just steps from the San Siro, Casa Milan is AC Milan's headquarters. The centerpiece for fans is the Mondo Milan Museum. The interactive experience highlights the most thrilling moments from club history. Hungry fans can grab a bite at the club's official restaurant. Whenever Milan is playing, home or away, the match is guaranteed to be on the restaurant's huge TV screens.

INDEX

ABOUT THE AUTHOR

Todd Kortemeier is a writer and editor from Minneapolis. A graduate of the University of Minnesota's School of Journalism and Mass Communication, he has written more than two dozen sports books for young people.